IN TO THE LIGHT

Sketches and expressions
by Danny Clarke

Dedicated to Emma

Published by Cottage Gallery Publications 1991
Huskar Cottage, South Yorkshire Buildings, Silkstone Common.
Near Barnsley. South Yorkshire. S75 4RJ.

Cover photography
John Marshall.

Cover design
G.D.C.

Graphic reproduction
A.C.D. Graphics, Cawthorne.

Special thanks to
Rob Hanna.
Dorothy Waddington.
Jean Blackburn.

Printed by
Print City High Street, Silkstone.

I.S.B.N. O 9518680 O 4

4 – 95

FOREWORD

Yet another one of Barnsley's famous son's emerges in one of his three hats –(I've enough with one!) Having known Danny for many years wearing two of them – his musical and artistic ones – it is an enjoyable honour to be asked to foreword this book which I found to be a fascinating read. Danny's skill to make an everyday happening a visual experience we can associate with through his picturesque writings will, I am sure, evoke memories and enjoyment to a wide spectrum of folk (including Umpires in white hats!)

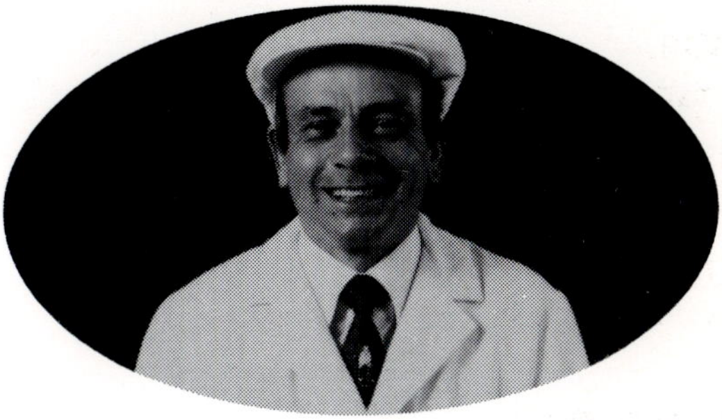

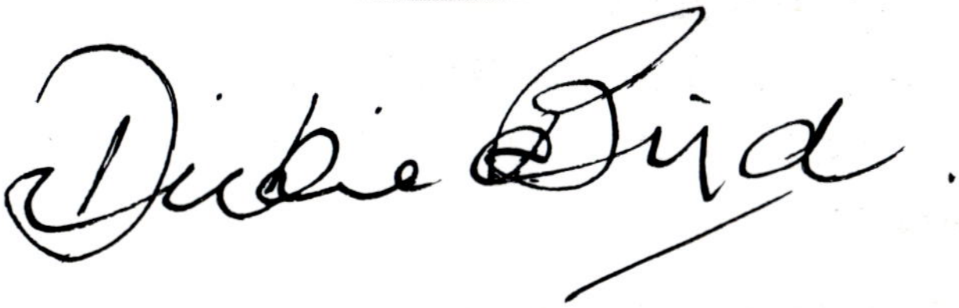

Harold 'Dickie' Bird M.B.E. is one of the most famous cricket umpires in the World–one of the game's greatest characters and author of many top selling cricket books.

LIST OF PHOTOGRAPH IMAGES

James Edward Clarke and Emma Hey 1928
and a late creation that followed

Darfield Road Juniors Football Team Cudworth
The teenage employment options in the area of the time were being a miner at Grimethorpe pit – working in the glass factory at Redfearns or Woods or become a professional footballer. Here we are all trying for the latter, a route taken earlier by local lad Mike Parkinson, though journalism was not on the agenda for secondary school leavers.

Mr Lowry outside his house the Elms said, "the house was everything I didn't want, too small, inconvenient for travel but moving would be too much trouble". I met him on the same doorstep.Six months before he died he gave me a friendly welcome and firm handshake and apologised for having to rush off and pay his electric bill. Painting through the night with one electric bulb was his studio situation for creating his work.

Emma Hey 1930's

Blackpool memorabilia – postcard and photos

1957 Isetta Bubblecar
Danny Dee and the Birdwell Rustlers
In typical Don Wallis 'Doncaster Studio'
Sixty Group Promotion Photo Pose'

Decca Record Press Photo for Foggy Dew–O
Royalty being 9d. from records costing 37/6d. in 1968 in
Company with The Rolling Stones and other starry–eyed hopefuls.

Sexy Sue on Market hill, Barnsley. (shirt by Frank Bird) *circa* 1969
Cover . Barnsley Main Colliery 1991.

ORDER OF VERSE.

ROGER McDANCE.
LAST TANGO IN OLDHAM.
EMILY R.I.P. – A.O.P.
THE TURN ON.
B'S AND BIRDS.
BEE IN THE BONNET.
BRIDGE CAT.
GIVE ME GALATA.
MOTORWAY THOUGHTS.
LOST SOCKS.
STREETS OF SHAME.

IN TO THE LIGHT.

WHAT AM I

Have you ever asked yourself the question
What am I
Where did I come from
And why
Silent beings ever continue accepting what is told
From a traditional age that withers
From preachings long grown old
So many things unanswered
Mysteries without a name
But, preoccupied with trivialities
Mankind ignores in shame:
With the father's seed
Sown in mother's field
The dawn of life begins
The quiet form is daily growing, tucked in nature's grace
And in time created flesh evolves as human life
This known, truth will accept
As human concept seen
So man and woman multiply
The catalyst is now
The being
Born to life without a choice
Likewise bound to die
The question still remains
What am I.

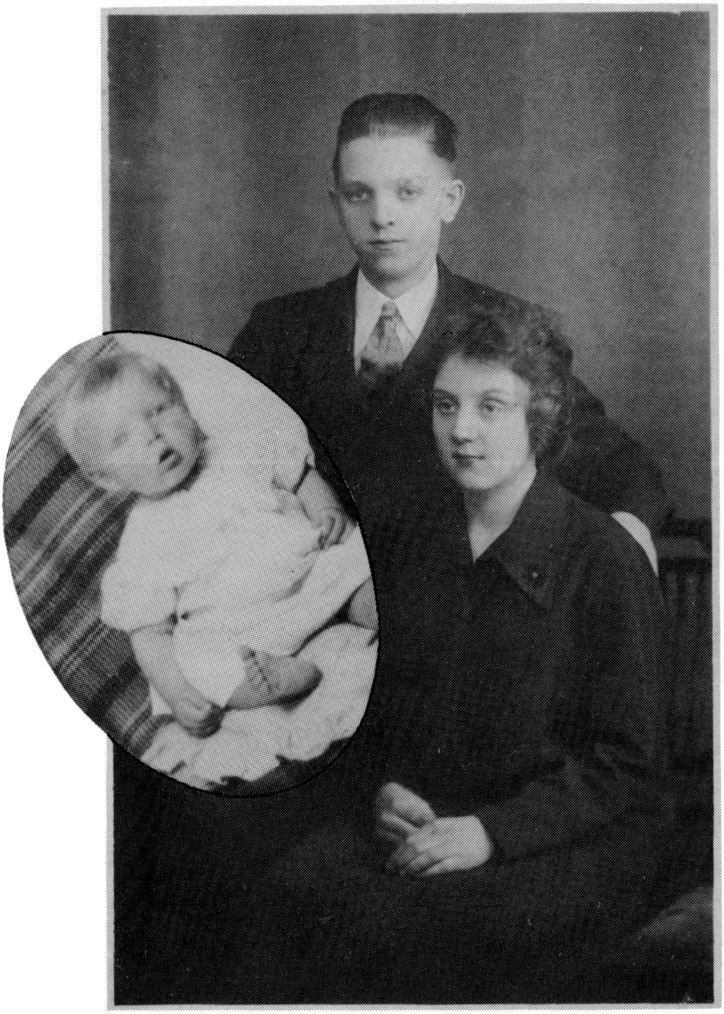

CHRISTMAS RE–VISITED

I could not sleep on Christmas Eve
My head was full of Christmas
Wherever that is
Children will wake soon
It's really their time
They are the ones who have the true spirit
And wide–eyed wonder
Whilst adulthood can only anaesthetise
Liquid fashion
The proof is even in the pudding
And eating your way out
Seems to be the answer
Along with the annual trail
Up the well–worn Church steps
On the path to peace
Joining the congregation
Fighting for the melody
Of the strange mis–matched tune
Some frustrated classical musician
Has decided to force upon the text
Of your once favourite traditional hymn
And struggling to associate
Valiantly mime the charade
Quietly praying for pub opening time to arrive

The last time I opened my eyes to Christmas
I was six
My eagerly awaited Christmas treasures
Turned out to be
An apple
An orange
A book
Some nuts
And just one real present
A wind–up gramophone
I can still remember
Seeing my father's ghostly figure
Silhouetted against the dawn light
His rotation arm working furiously
Intent on producing maximum effect
With my present
To be awakened with the rattle of George Formby
On his seventy eight
Describing the amazing delights
Derived from his employment in a Chinese laundry
Ironing ladies blouses
Was something very special
After careful instruction
Which probably qualified me
To mind a barrel organ for any given time
I was able to drive the gramophone for myself
And After careful mimicry

Do a scratching impression of my early musical hero
Giving joy which lingered for years

This year on Christmas day
I was awakened by
The incessant torturous pips of
Mr Simon and Mr Maniac
Computers
Making
Impersonal
Music at fingertip control
How do you impersonate a computer
No   Cancel
A computer impersonates you
Ojectively and without feeling
But has high interest level
Relative to battery power
Until breakage through misuse of object
Not made to generate a lasting impression ,and yet
The same wide–eyed wonder prevails
The spirit of Christmas
Is still alive and well in children
So be gone you cynical grown up
Jealously guarding your memories
Secretly wishing
That you could have another turn
At Christmas.

SAM CLARKE 1965 – 1977

Goodbye old Sam
Your days are gone
We could not save you
But we tried
The signs had been evident for a while
So the lump in my throat
wasn't quite as large as it would have been
had it come sudden
But I still had to leave the company
after it was done

My words were becoming incoherent
My eyes starting to swim
at first
I was going to leave you there
to be clinically disposed of
But
After feeling your soft warm fur
And seeing your eyes still open
despite the unfriendly needle
It seemed
I was deserting the cause

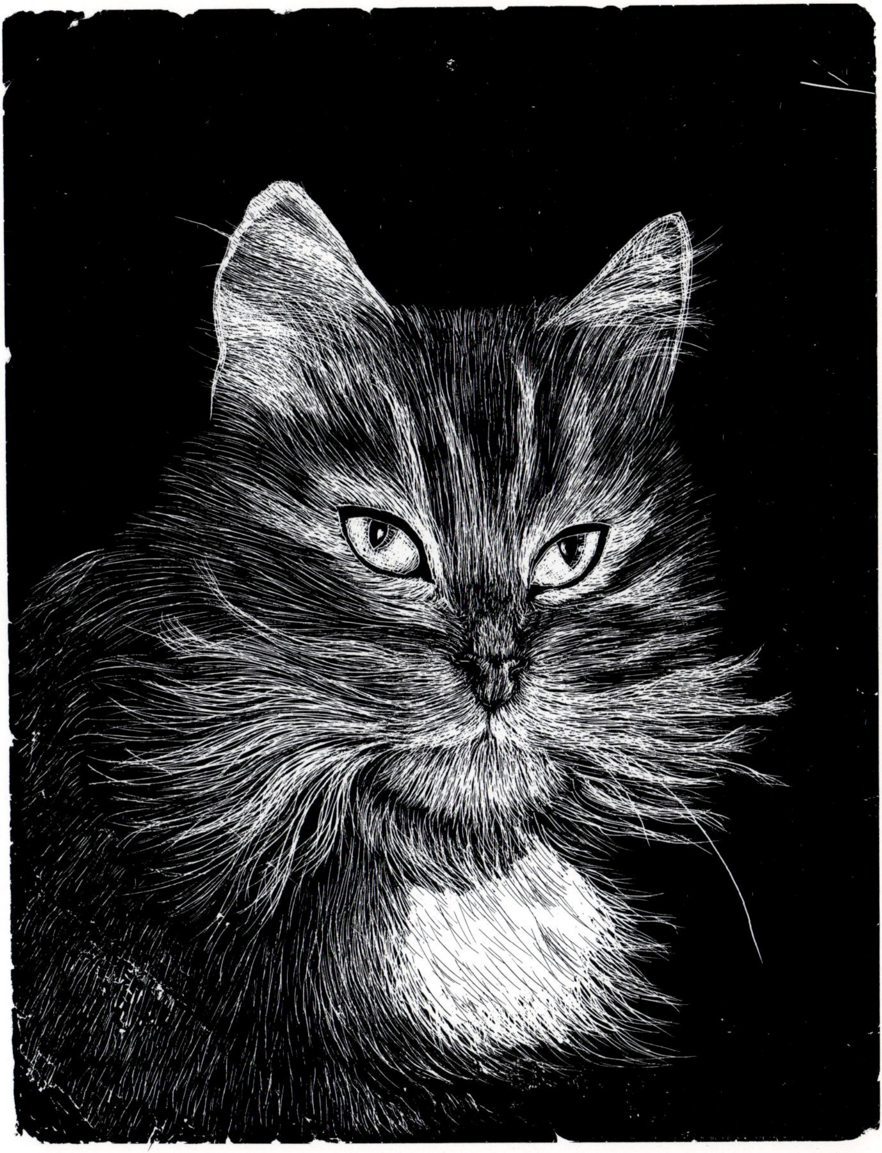

Twelve years on .....
after finding you covered in garage grease
Half dead from hunger
and unsuspecting motherhood
Into the shopping bag you went
Down the road to the big city
Barnsley

A new life
Transferred
from your garage corner box
and new found friends
Then you really started socialising
from Pop Stars to Politicians
Landladies and Electricians
Your captured the lot it was something you'd got
Perhaps – your eyes – like green saucers
and tortoiseshell fur
or maybe your controlled
aloof manner

I recall the time when I went away
you were locked in for days wi' nowt to do
But with one window appearance
and down trodden frown
You had folks feeding letter box
wi Kit–e–Kat all week
You were talk of 'Town

You got so friendly
You didn't know when to stop

So after kittens galore
Samantha got chop
They snipped out your glory box
at my own request
after working so hard
Thought it needed the rest
It gave you time to try
Acting ...

Embellish my songs
Trying to show people
Right things from wrongs
On our T.V. debut
The camera crew were impressed
But you just yawned on cue
and sailed through the test
You were seen in Cudworth
and throughout Yorkshireland
They remembered you at garage
Thought you were grand

"Ee's come a long way
since his motor trade days
Ee'll be growin' long 'air next
and 'aving pot smoking ways"

But Sam wasn't tempted
He just shrugged it all off
He was happy just being
the occasional Toff ...

He's still here at home
Sort of ... resting ... outside
He was still warm when I left him
I tried to be gentle
As if he was still there
Talking to him like a fool
in the cool evening air
I lowered him down slowly
then covered him up

It's no forest lawn
No medals – no cups
Just his favourite spot

Beneath the Rose and Lilac tree
Where he himself used to sit
And be
Outside my window
Though saddened to see
Helps me remember
Days of Sam and me.

Τэοωδ φυωιτβαλλ эυτ

It came all the way from Donny
Way back in '52
Members of Committee put up brass
They 'ad teams of golden 'eroes
In them days, did Darfield Road
And many went to National Class

It used to be a nissen 'ut, been used during war
And probably thought its days were done
Till lads from Cuderth came wi'offer
Then its real days begun

Duels that have since been fought around that 'ut
Would make its R.A.F. days seem tame
Especially when biguns from Doderth came
Then everybody went 'ome lame

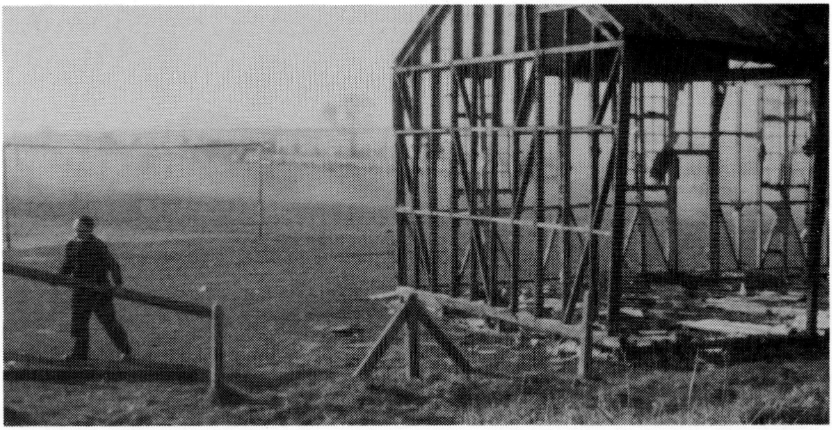

Its smelt a few ton of sawdust
No fancy marking gear 'ere
And the Saturday smell of dubbin and oil
Never mixed well with Friday night's beer

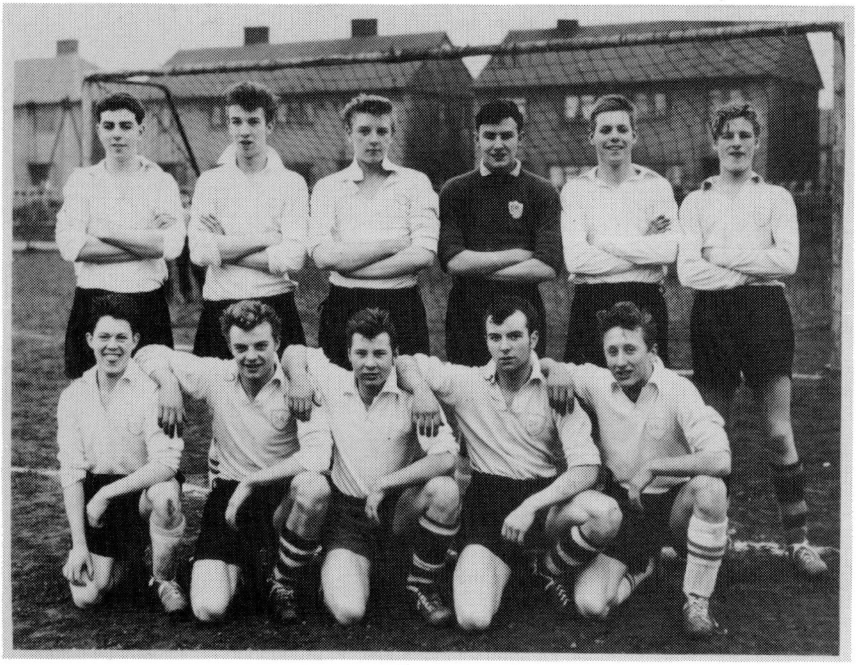

Photo by Courtesy of the Barnsley Chronicle

But cups were won and glories found
And praise showered upon
Then the long weekly wait–to–see what they'd said
If they 'ad in the Barnsley Chron

But sad to report despite all thats been
Its colourful life is no more
All that remains is a skeleton frame
Since vandals moved in with their score

But aerosol scrawls and the woodworm that mauls
Can't erase the memories stored
In the minds of the lads
Who followed their dads
Through that amazin' stuff
Fuwitball

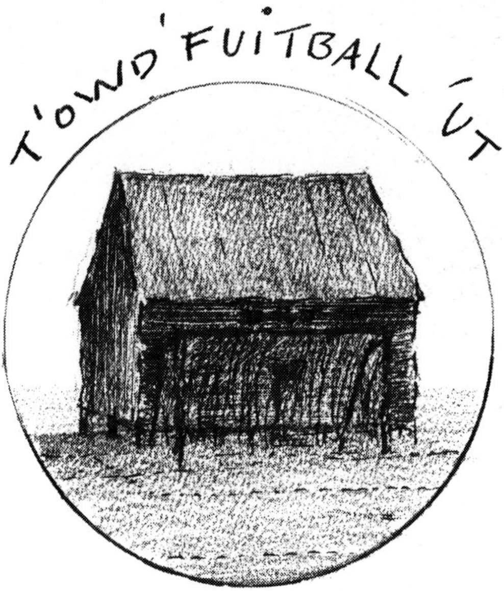

DOWN YOUR NECK ON PUB WEEKEND WALKABOUT

Real hail and hearty
Hand pulled and frothy
Gallons of nectar
Flowing from the depths
Through the system
To the ejaculating pump
Dripping down
The barmaids painted fingers
Into the slop tray
Recycling for tomorrow's
Cooked in beer menu

How specific
The gravitational pull
Is credited to the   ALE
                              M–ALE
                            FEM–ALE

Competing with the social round
                the musak sound
                home comfort ground

Is not questioned
On the pub weekend walkabout
With the second time rounders
For the lost and founders.

JOHN'S GONE

He went in his sleep last night
It was time to go
The cheer up smiles from visitors
Were becoming weary and waxwork
Tears finished ages ago
And everybody knew

Crabs are very nice
In the Pub over a pint
Or with mixed salad at home
But not when little sods are eating your neck
The great technological wizards are struggling
For the magic potion for this one

Bring on the screens nurse .....

The wobbly casters rumble
Over the wooden floor
Sounding like some hallowed death knell
Through the faded curtains
Gloomy lights cast a collage of shadows
That leap around
Projecting upward
On to the ceiling
Where they display themselves
Puppet theatre fashion
Involved in some bizarre ghostly dance

After the ball was over ...

The resident orchestra is in attendance
The oblivious flatulent snoring blanket Bulges Band
Invite you – to join them
In yet another Moonlight Saunter
Accompanied tonight by
The swishing swashing disinfectant dance team
Wafting around – on the air – competing
With death's strange unique odour

Hurried footsteps creep
Shorter
Tighter
Tenser
Whispered voices work
Hushed
Clearly
Closely together
Strains of lifting
Clearly
Precise

Not much weight on him
A lightweight burden
The wheels start to roll behind the screen
The screen wheels move adjacent
In perfect harmony with the internal trolley
A clever exercise in the art of obliteration
Using the two movable objects

A macabre piece of conjured magic
That didn't wait for any applause
The Band were still playing their trumpets
And I was the only audience

The show is over
As the rumbling wheels fade away
Down the corridor
Taking another predictable passenger
On his last ride
Not much of a glory trail
Not very heavenly at all
Not a saint in sight
Or angelic choir
No aerial cameras
Panning out
Wide and skyward
With rising orchestral volume and swell

Just
A squeaking trolley
And three gingham clad night nurses
Or was I looking the wrong way.

THE ELMS

Chris and Tex
are playing graffitti games
showing to all
they are here
at this neglected Victorian dwelling house
on bus route 237 – limited stop
It's the one with the old oil container
dumped on the doorstep
Castrol is best
but only when its full
The paintwork – faded blue–red
as once in Maroon
continues It's oxidized bloom
They didn't have many colours in those days
and he only used five
The stained glass window panel still survived
well sheltered
within it's protective oaken frame
Diamonds and squares
with angled line
Almost inviting
A de–luxe game
of noughts and crosses
On this sadly forgotten craftsmanship
Of another age

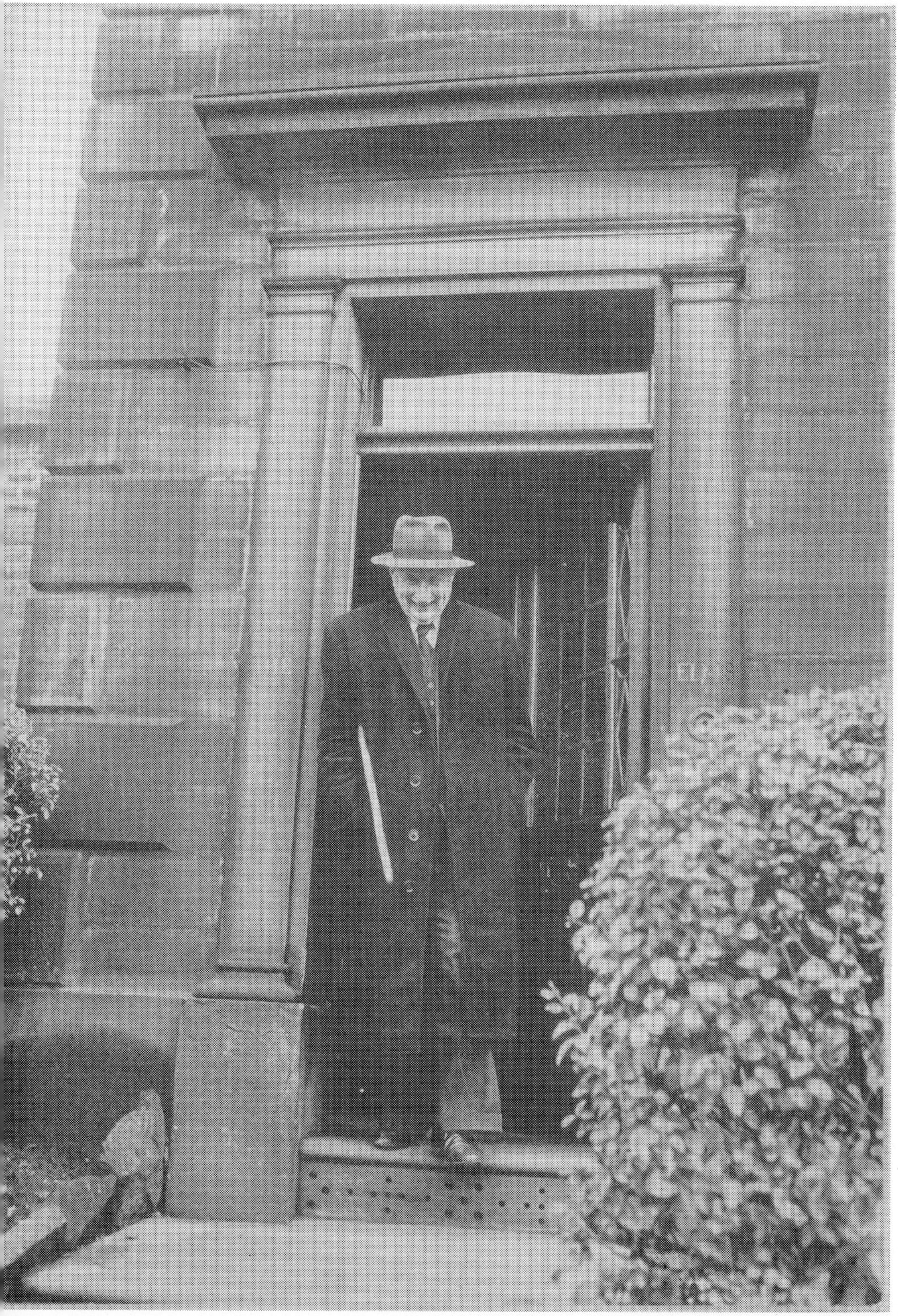

This house that once proudly showed itself
with its Greek influenced splendour
now struggles to reveal itself
from behind its weary overgrown hedge as the elms
Pollution and grime also appear
to be winning their battle
for supremacy over the condemned
Although the faithful adjacent tree still stands
sheltering stories
drawn from over a hundred seasonal years
now reluctantly sharing its roots
with the house next door
Recent mock Georgian
with matching plastic
and the nerve to ajoin its red–brick masonary
to the weathered stone of this once detached abode
Folks daily hobble past
hardly acknowledging its existence
apart from
Chris and Tex
who have finished painting their names
and have made a statement to the world
of their presence
Something
Mr Lowry
just managed in his twilight days
after living their for ages.

EMMA

I missed my mother's birthday yesterday
She's understand
I was always late for everything
So I played her favourite song on the piano
For her today
The flowers will come later
With roots
Not cut
She liked things to grow
So I'll plant this grave in Springtime

Come and find the place
Where I am lying – oh Danny Boy

The words echo on
From the many times
I'd listened to her merry version of the song
Inspired from being 'fresh' on guinness
The frequent remedy
For the drowning of sorrows
And the spirit
To live on

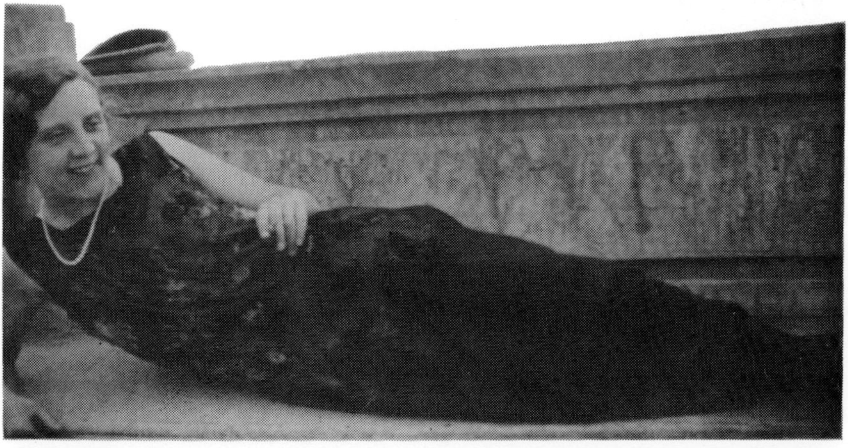

DAY – JAY – VOO – BLACKPOOL

Alice in Wonderland
Cries hopefully out
For all to see
The pleasures of her garden
And the clown
Laughs on

Its another rainy Blackpool morning
And you are going to enjoy yourself
We have spent a lot of money
Undaunted stallholders still force you to
Shoot the rabbit
Feed the duck
"Stick a dart in the card mister"
Or yourself – is this real?

The candy floss web is still spinning
Pablo still lures you in
To taste his real ice cream
To then drives you out
With his plastic hamburgers and smelly onions
Gipsy Rose (Mark III) is still reading palms
And displaying the faded photographs of the famous
That she and her sisters long since encountered

Michael Holiday and Gene Vincent
Must have visited on a grey day

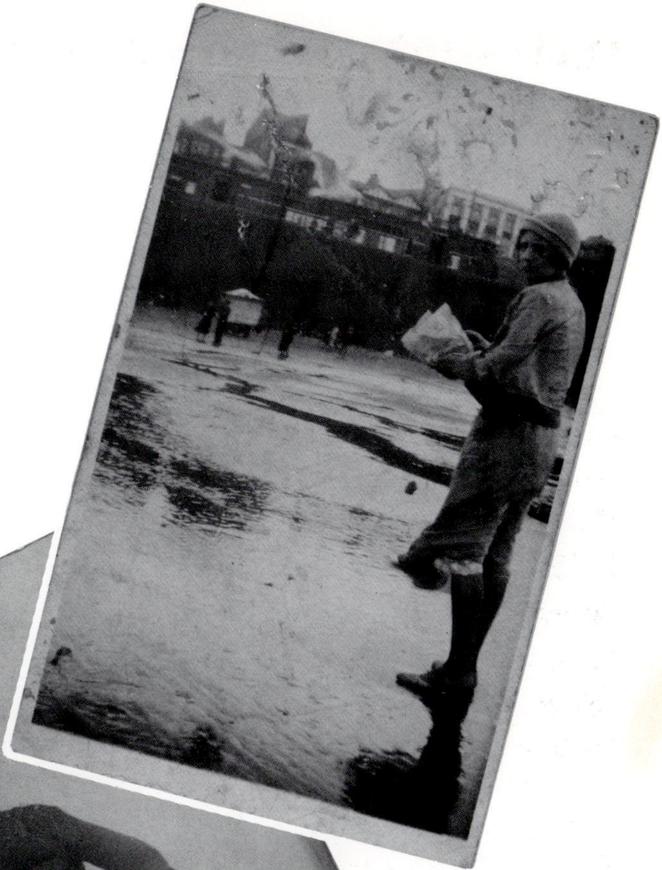

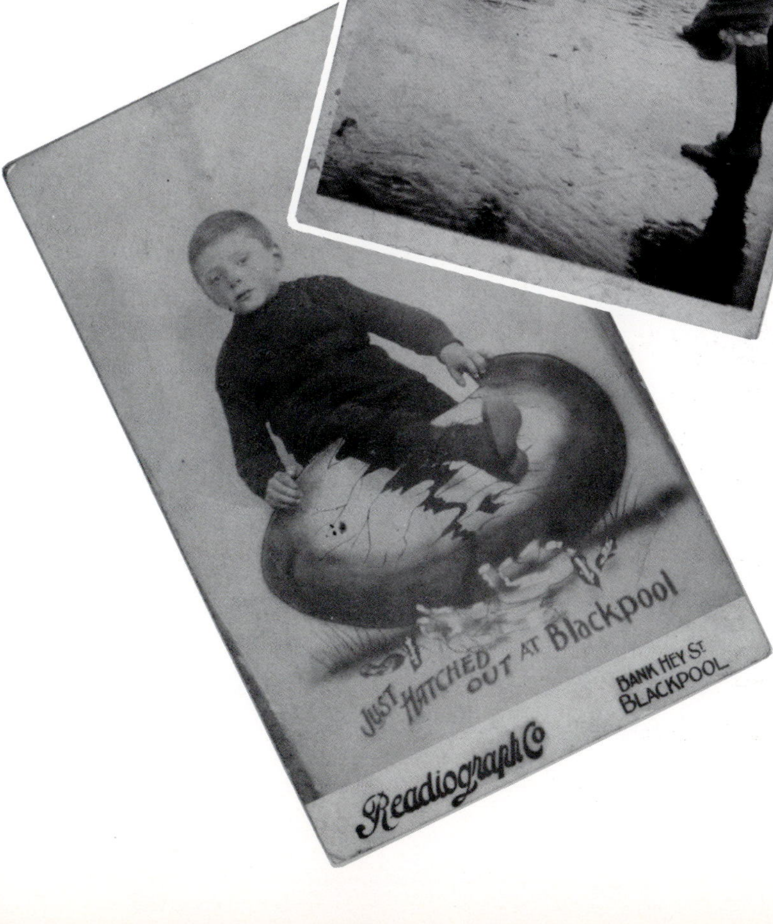
JUST HATCHED OUT AT Blackpool
BANK HEY ST. BLACKPOOL
Readiograph Co

Yate's Victoriana Lodge sups it's way along
Strangly looking like and old railway station bar
That's opened a few extra barrels
Due to a bit of surprise custom
Keeping all the male,
long pinafored waiters chasing around
Driving their handlebar moustaches with skilful ease

The Scottish invasion continues
Aggressive Glaswegians show off their tattoos
And demolish drinks
The cattle market has moved
The Tower lounge is no longer the place to espy and fantasize
Your prospective horizontal nourishment
Mama Jenks place has opened
And if it doesn't move
It's been painted purple
With drinks to match
Beer and Blackcurrant, Luv.

Stars are still in season
If you go down well
We'll book you again ...
The well aclaimed zenith of a showbiz career
A six months sentence at the end of a pier
London agents come to view
But miss the real entertainment

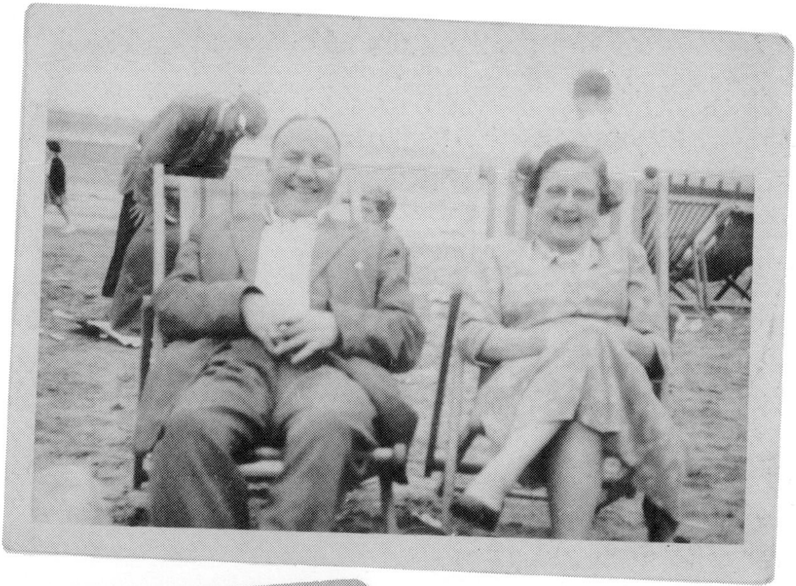

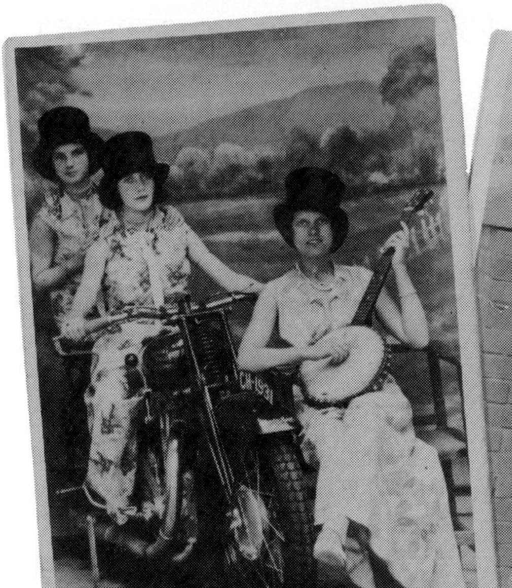

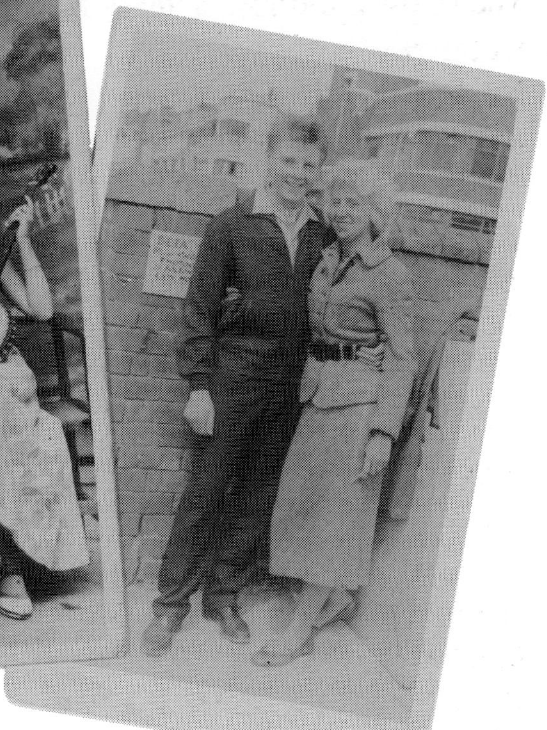

The enthusiasm and innocence of
Uncle Eddie's children's talent show
Free – twice daily
It steals the glory
But no–one sees except Mam and Dad
How sad

The mucky sea lashes in
Daring you to bathe in its polluted water
Better play safe
Occupy one square yard
At this over–crowded Derby baths
Hoping all are polite
With natures watery urges

I would be nice
To rise above all this
With a tower ascent
And trust a lift
That's had fifty years of savage trade
And sea abrasion

This strange uncanny progressive fusion
Blackpool – lives on
Only some of the names have been changed
To protect
The new unsuspectors.

CYCLING UP HILLS

I met a man in a pub who told me
I should pedal my bike up hills
like he does
to show young 'uns us owld 'uns
can lick 'em
I told him I made all the decisions
in my life affecting me
including uphill cycling.
He became more aggressive and
shot me a military stare
which I matched with perfect pacifism
he then turned on my drinking companions
saying I was drinking with old men
because I didn't cycle uphills.
I decided to compliment him
on his fitness and the superior quality
of his cycle with splendid uphill gears.
This seemed to defuse his aggression
Mr Macho returned to his serious drinking
and my friends got the colour
back in their faces.
I vowed to improve my fitness
and gear my bike and body
to uphill re–cycling
hoping one day to be a man
in a pub who can cycle up hills.

Dancing for Daddy

The graceful little lady
interprets the musical sounds
spontaneously on the lounge
carpet and Daddy looks
admiringly on.

Pavarotti and little Katy
make an incongruous
combination
of perfection with naivety
the mechanical with the live.

He entertains millions
she only three
especially Daddy
to the envy of millions
that weren't here
watching Katy
dancing for Daddy.

HE SAID – SHE SAID

He said yes
She said yes
It seemed
a good idea at the time
Everyone said
they were made for each other
It was
the expected thing to do
They couldn't let everyone down
After all
Presents had been collecting for ages
The bottom drawer was filled to the brim
And
His parents had a few bob anyway

The wedding was white
but they had slept together before
many a time
Never quite
getting it right
He came too quickly
She never came at all
So
They never went anywhere together

But
You can make babies in seconds

Anyway
They thought it would make a change
The social scene was becoming predictable
Affairs were becoming tiresome
And they
were starting to drift
So
Having kids
making families
brings things
together
A sense of belonging

It works
for a while
Like
having new toys
Until the novelty
wore thin
The unselfishness of parenthood
becoming a heavier burden
than the marriage

And
After tears in the night
both saw the light
So
He said yes
and she said yes
It was the only thing to do
Face mistakes
Legally
Share
For the first time
Only
Down the middle
Apart
from the children
who should work out
at weekends
Arrangements will work
They'll have to do
Alternatives don't exist anymore
She took the paintings ....He took the clock ....
The carpet went back ....It was bought on the knock ....
Knock for knock blow for blow ....
Lasted forever
The bickering game
Until he mentally snapped
and hit her again
She called the police

She scars were deep
Collapsed on the stairs
A fallen heap ....
How could it get to this
They almost loved once
So he said yes
and she agreed
Goodbye.

SECRET AFFAIR

We all need our secrets
Can't give everything away
Save something
For yourself
Being to ourselves
The most important thing in our lives
Why share with others
What's yours
Unless
Yours isn't a secret on its own
Until it comes together
With someone else's secret
But then –
It's not a secret anymore
So don't feel guilty.

DIVORCED –ABOVE IT ALL

I lodge in hiding
Nursing the scars of betrayal
Alone
In the roof
Like a bat In hell
Welcome to coventry
And the ex–step family
Who cleverly switch
To the deaf–mute button
With two–faced comfort
And ease
Whilst the paper parasites
Solicit
And do as required
Within the system
Where legal deeds reign supreme
Over truth and reality
As the years of my life are taken
And sucked dry
For ambition and greed
By the misguided cannibal
In pursuit of her second–hand dreams
And my first nightmare
Both without the comfort
of sleep.

THE SELL–BY DATE

The Hospital rang
Harold died
this morning
Your divorce papers are on the shelf
she calmly informed me

There there
she said
in mock comfort
as I burst into tears
It was for the best
It will be alright ....

Harold my step–father
was dead
He was brain–drained
It was for the best
She decided our marriage
was dead
and had been secretly
digging my grave for ages
And I
was also shelved
and laid to rest.

THE BUBBLE

I'm bubbling
Under the charts
he said
with a confident air
Well
Me and my group
His moonface beamed radiantly
Like a delighted football pools winner
Only
His game
was still being played
And
His bubble
had yet to burst

The wild expectancy
of his blind youth
aroused thoughts
of my own
previous naivety

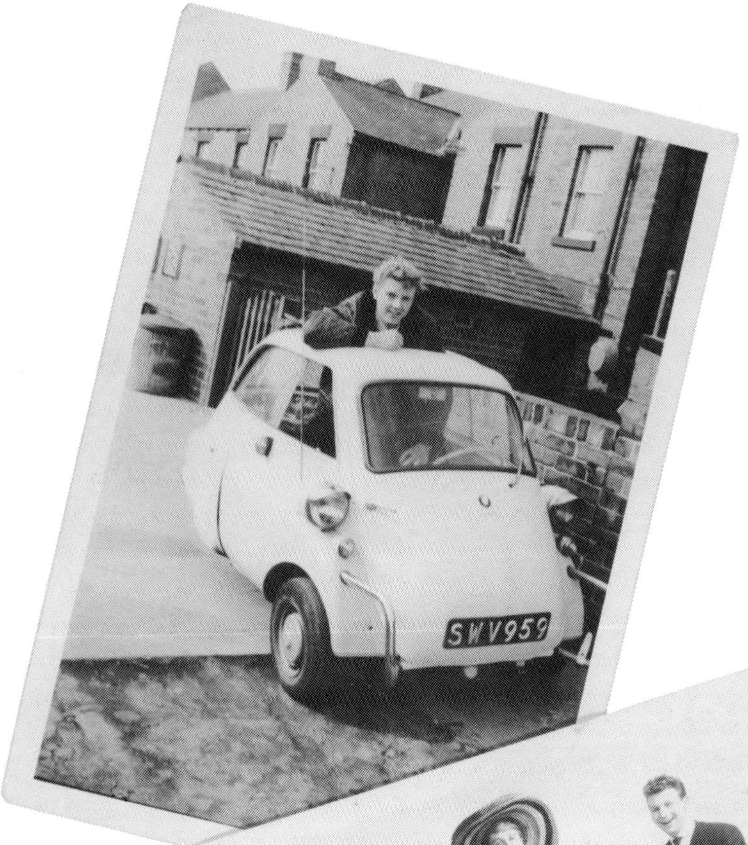
SWV959

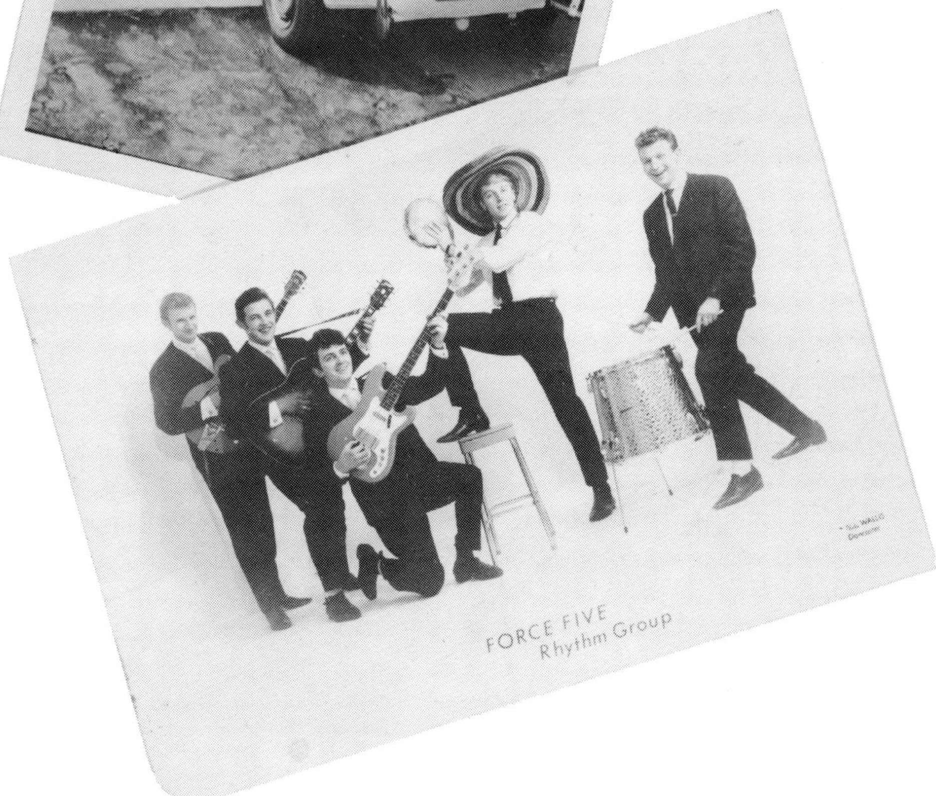
FORCE FIVE
Rhythm Group

To remenisce
My record release
In tin–pan alley
Which had
high hopes
for the hit parade
Spins on turntables
on wireless light programmes
Thanking our lucky stars

We managed to catch
The six–five special
So lookout
Alma Cogan Russ Conway
and the rest of the cornball
American plagarists
I'm going to bubble
So big
So big
And burst – and burst and –
Did anyone see
Where my bubble burst.

P.S. THANKS

Tonight I saw Paul Simon
He was smaller than I thought
But that was only his size
His songs and music were as big
as you can get them in '91 –
The American dream has happened
after thirty years on from carefree College
days of '58 when two young hopefuls
called themselves Tom and Jerry
Copied the Everly's – with more
enthuasiasm than skill – before
they eventually successfulled and Garfunkeld
But not before he got lost in Lancashire
in downtown Widnes ,Inspiring homeward bound
on his way to the Essex flat Landscape
and polite Brentwood
Where his love lied – waiting silently for him
with the twelve pounds inclusive fee in his pocket
the going rate for an hour of the Simon sound
in a time when
you could be Foggy–Dew–O'd for fifteen pounds
and David Bowied for eight
A time of innocence   A time of comfort
Preserve your memories they're all that's left you
they all come rushing back tonight
when I saw big **P**aul **S**imon.

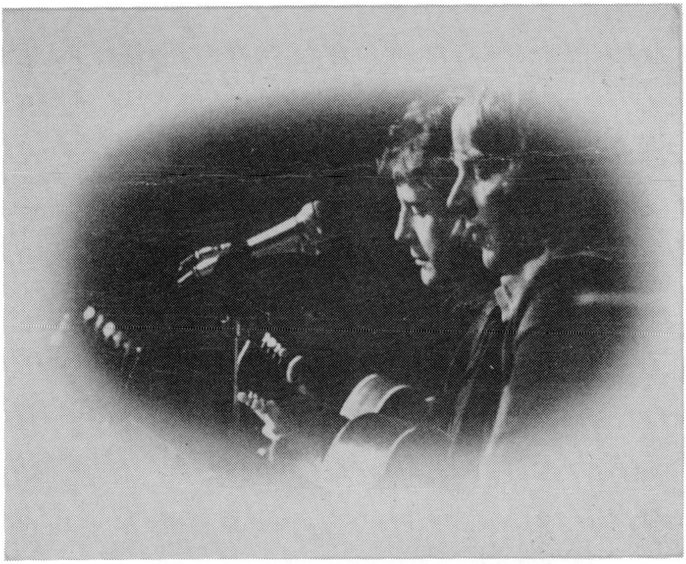

THE FOGGY DEW-O

Decca Records

NO ONE REALLY MEANS IT ANYWAY

Take it from the top of the scene
Okay
Here we go
Quiet please
In five
And cue .....

Action starts
The telephone rings
Another TV drama
From the makers of Kings
And Queens
Lines are spoken
Following the herd
It's only acting

And a little absurd
And no–one really means it anyway
Today's face fits – for only a while
The toothpaste grin
The plastic smile
The agents sell
With all the style
And no–one really means it anyway

TV is such a hungry machine
Eats people
Contracts
And lonely has beens
Occasionally loved
But most obscene
And no one really means it anyway

The jostling extras
Jockey for placing
A prominent place
Or anything facing
The camera's eye
To start careers racing
But it doesn't really mean much anyway

The charade continues
Pretentiously keen
Impressing the in–crowd
Joining the team
Goodbye values
Idealistic dreams
I'm in the machine
I'm in the mach
I'm in the ma
I'm in th
I'm in
I'm
I.

BRITTANIA RULES AT THE END OF THE PIER

A hundred years out
into the cold North Sea
stands an eroding platform
For hopeful dreamers
and showbiz schemers
Where rooms are wallpapered
with faded dog–eared posters
of the once famous
slowly sinking toward twilight oblivion
Whilst today's talent
soldiers onward
Armed with
Dreams
Equity contract
And blind faith
On the same well trodden boards
Where
The yesterstars did it
For much less
Donovan the singing poet
Dylan–cloved
For five shillings
Harry
was Worth

And did it
for nine and sixpence
While others
were available
at popular prices
Tonight's unpopular price
is seven pounds fifty
Yet
All bums are on
all seats
As today's stars
Cannon Ball their way
Through the last night
of the long Summer season
With merry japes
Special thanks
The flowers
and the parting glass
The goodbyes
The Exodus
After riding the waves
So long
The terra
Seems firma than ever
and Northern thoughts
are sweeter than ever
on the road homeward.

SEASIDE AWAY FROM IT ALL

A painted woman
eats ice–cream
through her lipstick face
Her husband
proudly sports his latest pair of braces
Over–emphasising
his over–fed paunch
which lazily rests on the pay–out counter
of the amusement machine
that he also continually feeds

Nothing like a good holiday
does you good to get away from it all
Away from it all
Averting my eyes
to the opposite backdrop – as –

Seabirds fly
in a white cluster
across the sea
Then come back to land
like a descending diamond necklace

F
A
L
L

I
N
G

On blue velvet

The ocean
works increasingly on
Bringing
seaweed from Sweden
fishes from France
more sand for the children
to build castles
and dance

Ornament fossils
long buried with time
Now there
at the surface
washed back
with the grime

Sounds of a steamer
back from foreign domain
with cargo
and limpits
that cling
to their frame

Such wonder
The cycles of nature
on their majestic routes

Go
Sadly unoticed
by the lipstick lady
Who
By now
Has devoured her ice–cream
and left
With that man
To catch
the Bingo session
in the Pub

It does you good
To get away
From it all.

THE MYSTERIOUS GARDENER

A small seed
Was planted
And it grew – tall – high – wide

But there was confusion
Over the gardener's name
And where the seed came from

He is supposed to answer to God
But he has many names
Depending where your seed grows
And how it flowers

Not all bear fruit
Some are poisonous
And take strong root
To strangle the delicate
And the gardener cannot be found
No matter what name is called

The only logical assumption
Has to be
That to start a garden
You need
Seed
Water
And earth.

THE GAME

And the crowd asked their leaders
What are we fighting for
For what purpose and why
And they were told
For freedom
And the making of peace
But
That is what the enemy
Are fighting for
As well
Answered the crowd
And there was silence from their leaders.

THE FIGHT

He made a club – they made a knife
He made an axe – to save his life
He made a bow and arrow – as they made a spear
So he made a suit of armour
To shield his fear
Then came the cannon
Then came the gun
Exploded the rocket
Exploded the bomb
And then they were gone
And
Then
They
Were .

JOCKSTRAP AND CRICKETGUARDS

Jock straps and cricket guards
fall from my wardrobe
as I search through yesterday's clothes
for last year's Summer shorts
Jaded from life in the fast lane
Trying to find space and sunshine
An escape from cackling neighbours
Out in force today
Dressed in bell tent dresses
disguising their unhealthy eating habits
And the women are even worse
Talking – saying nothing
Emitting a decibel level
Generated from a history
of competing against the noisy factory machines
of industry past
The machines now silent
Yet people shout on
Refusing to acknowledge
the industry is finished
Or all other ears within a 1OO yard radius
are not interested in listening to their banal drivel
and it's foreign dialect tones
with its tha "nose"

Quaint Barnsley English to some
A comforting togetherness of class to others
and a personal reminder to myself
of my victimised early years
For having the nerve to be something
other than indigenous cannon–fodder
For pit or bottle factory
and needing more
than a jock strap or cricket guard
For protection.

For young people who have accidents in cars

But these are only words
as the grass now trodden under foot
given time will rise again
like the Phoenix from the ashes of pain
The flower will return to bloom
brighter than ever
but for now be brave, have faith,
trust and love from within
and here my gift from the outside
but they are only words.

HAVE YOU HAD IT BEFORE

I confessed that I had
In 1969 – forget the nineteen
My intended freudian mind game pun
Fell on deaf ears, her piercing stare said all
We get 'em all in here
Sit down – and fill in this form – buster
And state all associations with
Men's bottoms
Aids
Dirty women
Aids
Contemporary diseases
Jeremy Beadle –
You have 3O seconds starting from
Give me your hand – prick the thumb
Pump up the arm – give me a gland
Stick a hole in your skin
Pint of best red – coming up – dripping down
The Dracula's Arms – open all hours
Come
Liedown – the woman said
Could this be 69?
No
Just a cup of tea and a biscuit
A comforting aid
For blood donor lifesavers.

MR AND MRS POSTMAN

I've lost my love
To a postman
He obviously delivered
Everything I didn't
His early rising
His stamp of approval
Must have influenced
My removal
His post
His sackful
His out–fit
His in–pull
My second class service
Against his first class delivery
She and he
Met
Married
Made baby in six weeks
What speed
What service
But then
There are other letters to embrace
Which eliminate
Delivery.

Lucy Launderette

Lucy Launderette a washing goes
a powdering her dirty clothes
feeds the glass eye
sends it spinning
sails away for just one shilling
Mary's panties – 'erberts drawers
enraptured together
without a pause
light goes out at journeys end
the tangled heap now left to tend
one–eyed monster mouth goodbye
Thanks a lot–now off to dry

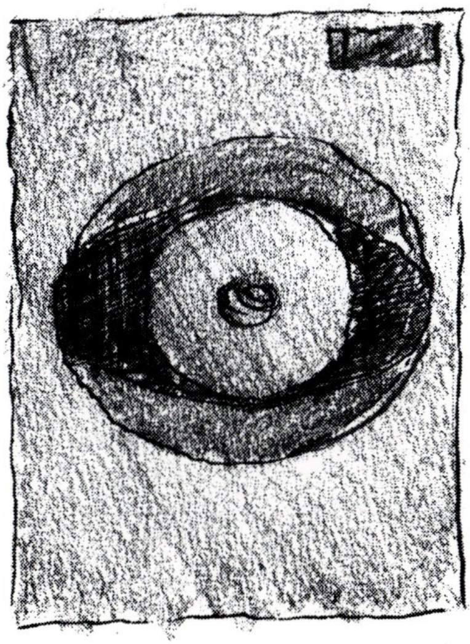

P.A.Y.E. (pay as you learn)

Friday evening – Has extra meaning
From daily working – To weekend shirking
Meeting, waiting – Transportating

Collecting each – Loving peach
With monthly cheques – For equal sex
Together parked – By supermarked
Noisy clatter – Friendly natter
Choosing food – For Sundays' mood
Traffic slowly – Drags unholy
Eventual urban – Detached suburban
A Jones' estate – Cheap mortgate rate
Slippers found – With faithful hound
Sink to chair – One of T.V. pair
Food intaken – Now left to waken
To dream of hols – On Costa del Sols

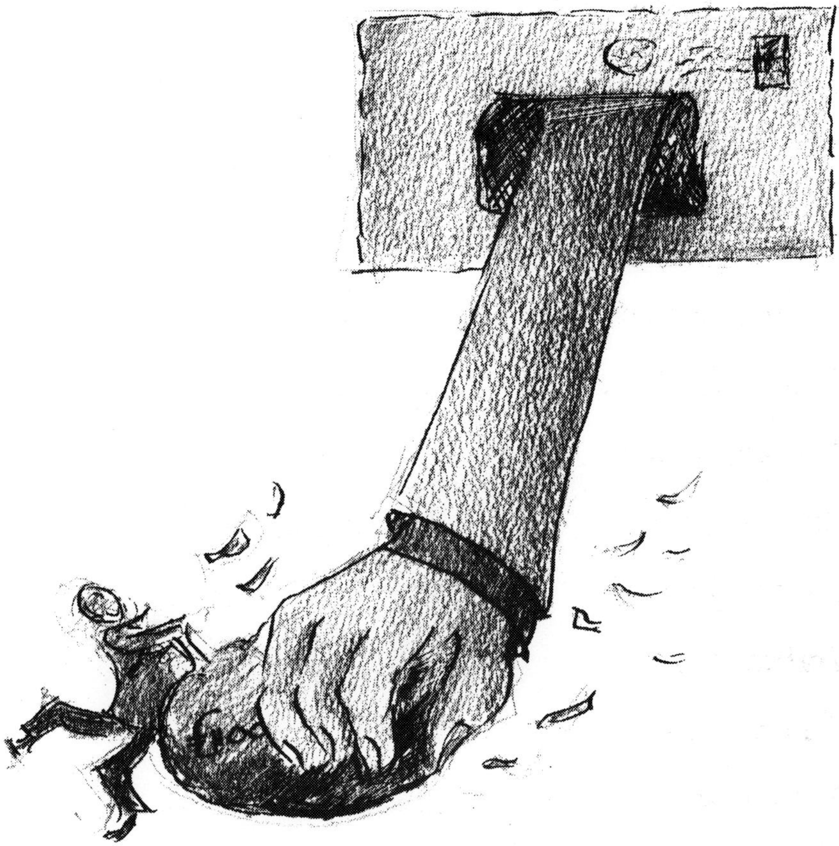

Dear Mr Average,

The Government thanks you for your support
But each racket does not carry a wealth warning .....

SYD AND GERALDINE

I know Syd and Geraldine
But I've never really spoken
Just seen them in the car wash
Fumbling ....
With his token

She sits on the left
He is on the right
Unless you look from the back
Or passing in the night
When

Their shrines become
A love nest
Entwined
Changing
Displacing
Positions don't seem to matter then
They don't care which way they're facing

But Syd intends his love is true
Thats why
He's stuck her
On the screen
To tell the world
He loves his car
Together with Geraldine.

STARTING AGAIN

Starting again
Ten years on
Ten years gone
I wrote a poem about
Your first mistake
Now
Here I am
Seen by you
As your second
Divorce is simple
Ask any Solicitor
Fifty per cent
Of today's blind faith matrimonials
End up
Starting again
While this confused statistic
Still wades through
The collected paper memories
And photographed Christmas smiles
Link letters
And cards of good hope
When I have the courage
To throw them all away
I'll know
I've really
Started again.

ROGER Mc*DANCE*

Roger a nimble fleet–footed lad
merrily eightsome reels
at Village Halls
Bi–focaled and bearded
this bi–spectacled giant
struts like a bold–peacock
all evening – impressing the
matronly gathering with his
whirling Kitty and low–flying sporran.
Eventually – this perspiring little flurry
settles his feathers and comes to roost
amongst his audience to receive his
acclaim – then changing his wee–bootees
into his 'He–man Clark Sole Treckers
and clutching his Chelsea Girl carrier
he – and his heavy tartan legs slime
off into the night – not before refusing
all offers of the Sheriff's job' – as his work
here is now finished – he has new horizons
to capture – converting English to Scots
for the Sheffield branch of Hypers and Pipers
Society – beware he could be
in your area soon.

LAST TANGO IN OLDHAM

A hundred permanent waves
sweep across
the polished floor
Delicate shuffling sounds
wisp along
to orchestral gramaphone tempos
of well remembered melodies
stepping out in time
on this afternoon reverie
of Lingering Blues
Dutifully preserved
by those well manicured partners
on parade
at the Civic Hall Tea Dance.

EMILY R.I.P. O.A.P.

Little white–sticked ladies
Passing by
The family wealth seen hanging from their
ageing golden frames
Fading by the seaside
While they have the time
Taking tea on the terrace
Reminiscing royal days
Like vintage crows settled comfortably
Upon their well feathered nests
While relatives hover like vultures
Ready to pounce and scavenge upon the
victim's eventual spreading fortune
Once Emily has breathed her last....
But Emily is smiling
For she knows whome she will g ive to
And knows what she will live for
How long she will stay
Then she'll fly away.

THE TURN ON

My hand
Groped around
In the darkness
Searching for light
My fingers
Eventually find
The bedside table lamp

I touch
The rim of the shade
Then
Swoop underneath
Diving
To its central force
To activate
To switch on

You never wear dresses these days
Your always harnessed
In spray on trousers
And repulsive tights
That cling
To form an armour of chastity
Gone are the days
When
A young man
Could get his vertical delight
In dusty doorways
Without removing a single item of clothing
The blind mystery
The adventure

And now
As I slide into bed
Alongside your sleeping naked body
I can only remember the days
When both our lights
Were turned on.

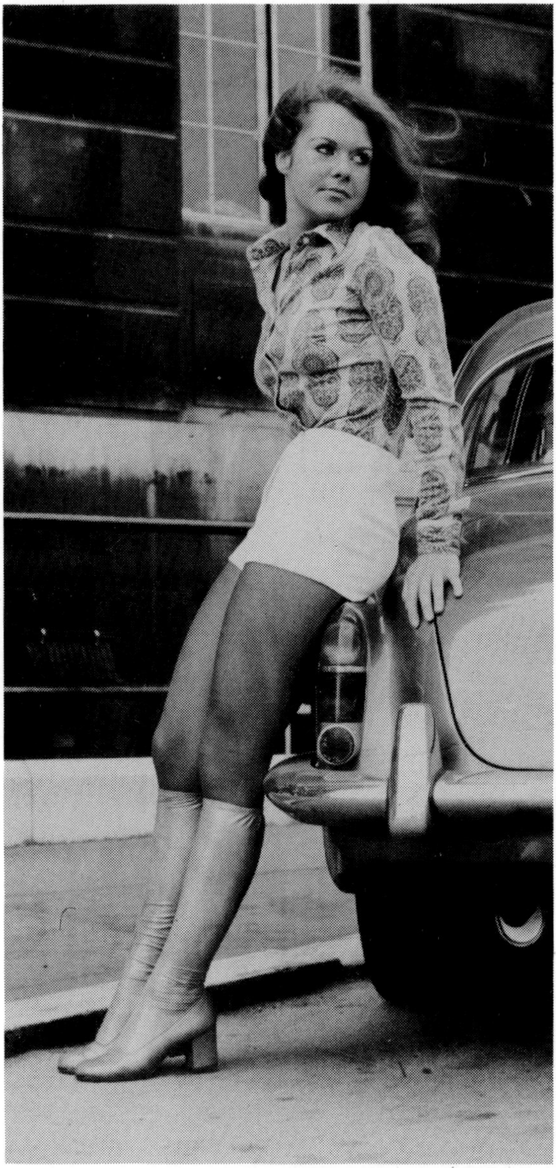

B's AND BIRDS

When all the world around you
Gets a bit too much to take
Just come with me
Not that other Silly B
And see
How much honey
We make.

The Bee in the Bonnet

The industrious bee
disappears
down another
snapdragon's mouth
and rumbles around
filling his ankle socks
with pollen gold
a prisoner of the hive
trying to please the Queen

The hard working lion tamer
enters the cage
and nochalantly places his brylcreamed head
in the circus lions mouth
and prays
for animal understanding
wishing sometimes
he was a Bee.

Bridge Cat

I said hello
To the cat
On the bridge
With my left over fish lunch
It pleased for more
With its well–rehearsed grin
It knew all the tourist tricks
Brushing its tail across my legs
Rhythmically pounding my feet
Playing me like a harmonium
But I realise that I'm really
Just another fishy tourist
A fleeting paramour
Yet still succumb
To the feline charm
As Turkish locals
Scorn the existence
Of bridge cat
Despite its rodent prowess
And re–cycling qualities
But then
I'v never had an aversion
To Persian.

Give me Galata

Goodbye Istanbul
and Galata the magnificent
bridgeing the centuries
providing life-blood
for its hundred floating traders
smoking and joking
amongst the smelly delights
where street-wise cats prowl
for the constant dish
of left-over fish
tossed from the table
caught by the able
sea-reapers proudly show
their catch of silver darlings
still feeding the flock
ensuring all remain and survive
on the bridge - times past and now
shabby clothed Turkish traders
loom from the shadows
hubbly-bubbling "best price for English"
my clothes touristical
far Istanbul the mystical
drenched in an Ottoman empire
of treasures and pleasures
especially Galata the Bridge.

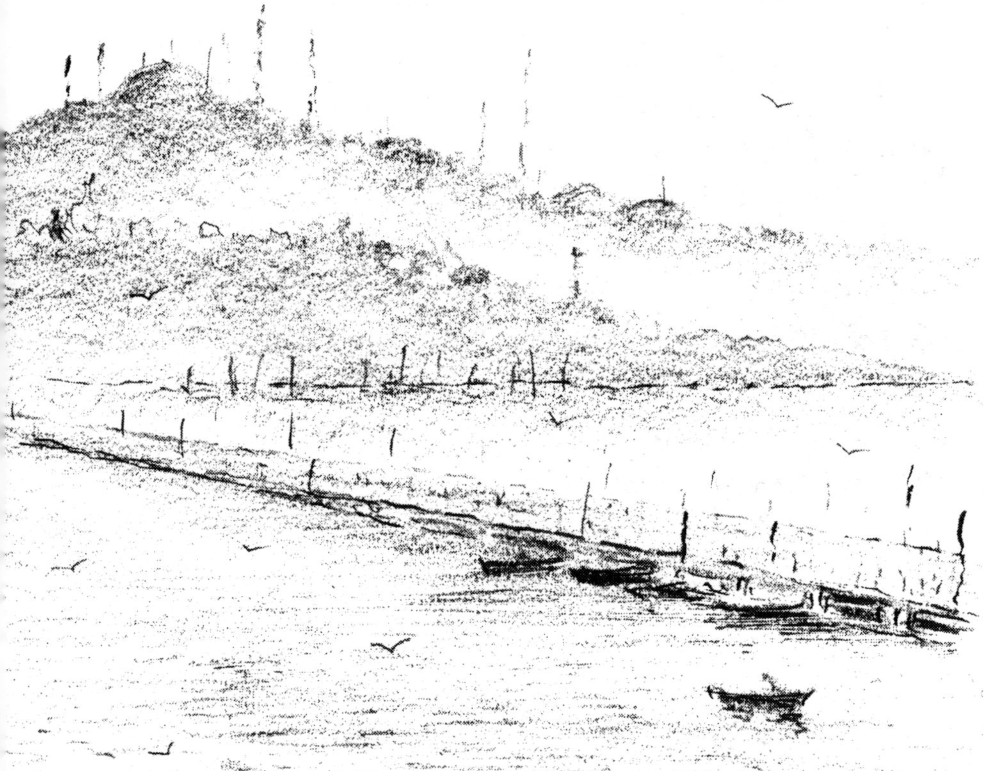

Moterway Thoughts

Times remembered
when love was new
The roadside place
whene teasles grew
that we collected for
decorative living room
corners and
a building of togetherness
and growing

Ten years on
we collect
seperately - papers
evidence of existence
furnishing the Law
with ammunition
to fire across it's
Courtrooms
painting undecorative
smears - over the years

But the teasles are still growing

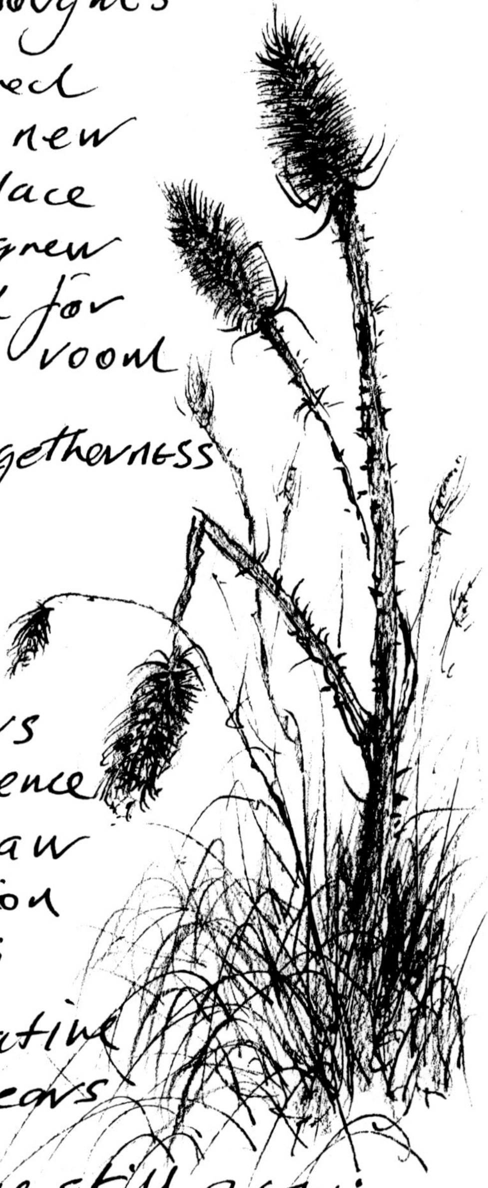

LOST STOCKS

So sad and lonely
So religious and holy
So crumpled
So down
My lost socks

Where are they now?
Have they been unfaithful
Are they going round with another 'foot'
Are they happy
My lost socks

I have eighteen single foot families now
after re–uniting three lost souls today –
they've probably had a little reunion celebration
in their bottom drawer
Who can blame them
My lost socks

Some aren't so lucky
Some get itchy feet
and sail off –
down the drain pipe trail
In pursuit
Of their dream
For bigger feet

Others get caught
In their mechanics of life
And are left
In a tangled heap
Round the washing machine cylinder
Poked and prodded
Experiencing hotpoint
At the end of a screwdriver
Whilst others are condemned
Locked in
With the discarded machine
On some dirty tip
Alone
Eventually crushed
Into sock oblivion
To rot back
From whence they came
To feed the ground
To grow the grass
Feeding wool sheep
Replacing
My lost socks.

STREETS OF SHAME

Religion smiles down from its elated throne
Covered in gold, ornate and opulent
The people look up from their ragged rugs of prayer
Weary from survival on a shoe string
Without shoes
And sometimes feet
Lamed and maimed at birth
By desperate parents
For richer street begging
Blind babies do well from the tourist
And the Gods still smile

Mother and daughter
Are forced into the cages of sin
Selling their flesh
To pay off family debts
On the streets of shame
This male–dominated state says
It should be so
And the Gods
Look the other way
And rupees rule
O.K.

Above the Hanging Gardens of Bombay
The Parsee burial tower provides another human flesh feast
To its resident vultures
So the land will not be soiled with rotting human carcass
Leaving the bones – to be ground into top soil dressing
And scattered on the earth
Feeding India on
Free faith
Religion
And smiles
And a vision
To see beyond
And rise into the outstretched arms of Heaven
Free from this hell on earth
Released
From the street of shame.

IN TO THE LIGHT

Creativity is all around us

Travelling on the air

Looking for somewhere to land

The body breathes it

The eyes take the photograph

The mind interprets

Collecting seeds of promise

To nourish with elements

For eventual flowering

In to the light.

Acknowledgments of friendships and influence

Clara Houldsworth William Blake Mike Hope Judy Collins Robert and Bridget Jones Ralph McTell Alan Wood Jack and Hedley Salt Lenny Wesley John Lane McTavishes Kitchens Peggy Rushton Tony Broadhead Stan Richards Alan Critchley Ann Dex Bach Ian Masters Tony Capstick Jim Badics L.S Lowry Geraldine Thewlis Ken Favel Ronnie Glavin Mike Ryal Matthews Bros. Sister Gabriel The Limelighters The Beatles Roy Lodge Desmond Curry John Stewart Joyce B Ellen Palshis Christine K Professor Peter McKellar Marianne Segal Harry Chapin June Crane Colin Hindmarsh Peter & Jo Simmonite Paul Simon Jacqueline Chadwick Evette Davis Buddy Holly Pete Clark Cherry Greaves David Llewellin Ruth Pitman Tom & Claire Horsefield George Spruce Jean Fisher Vance Arnold Paco–Bell T.S. Elliott Vic Mason Horace Crowther Veronica McSwiney Don McLean Nina Kascwicza Joe Scarborough Marianne Anderson Tom Paxton Erica Baker Isla St Clair Ian Kennedy Turner Dave Cousins Sandra Shirley Fuller William Russell Flint Paul McGann Lonnie Donegan Steve Rhodes Elvis Presley Beverley Coles Harry and Gail Deila Diana Bates Peter Shelley Brian Willoughby Bill Bracken Jo & Brian Austin Harold Mallinson Bobby Ball The Hanna Family Len Green H.R.H. Prince Charles Patsy and Ian Ashley Jackson Sandra Chambers Margaret Hope Mike Parkinson Salvador Dali Pete Seeger Spike Millighan and probably more.